**YOU AND YOUR "SENIOR MOMENTS"
- SO WHY ARE WE HERE?**

The sale of this book without its cover is unauthorized. If you purchase this book without a cover, you should be aware that it was reported to the publisher as "unsold and destroyed". Neither the author nor the publisher has received payment for the sale of this "stripped book".

DISCLAIMER
This cartoon book of senior citizens' reactions to life is purely fictional and is not directed at any one person or persons living or dead. The names, places and incidents are purely fictional and are the products of both authors imagination. Any resemblance to actual events, locals, persons, names of places or events is entirely coincidental.

This book is published by Bee Publishing Company at 429 East 83rd Street, 3A, New York, NY 10028.

Copyright © 2001 Edgar J. Schoen Jr. for editorial
Copyright © 2001 Paul Rossini for all illustrations
All rights are reserved.

No part of this book may be reproduced or transmitted in any form or by any means, electronic or mechanical, including photocopying, recording, or by any information storage and retrieval system, without written permission of the Publisher, except where permitted by law. For information address: Bee Publishing Company, 429 East 83rd Street, 3A, New York, NY 10028.

ISBN#: 0-9711277-0-0

First printing: 2001

Printed by: McNaughton & Gunn, Inc.

Library of Congress Control Number 2001130654

Printed in the United States of America

This book was digitally produced by Patti Courville.

Our thanks go to both our wives, Mary Lee Schoen and Cynthia Rossini for their patience during the many hours both authors spent in putting this book together.

We also thank whomever let us live long enough to be able to describe our memories of days gone by while also being able to put together cartoons and memories representing some of our thoughts.

EACH GENERATION IS GIVEN FIVE STAGES OF LIFE

The five stages of life are:
1) **PRE-TEEN YEARS**
2) **TEEN YEARS**
3) **YOUNG ADULT YEARS**
4) **MIDDLE AGE**
5) **OLD AGE**

STAGE 1

My pre-teen years were the years that some phrases stood out very strongly in my memory. Those phrases were, "do this", "do that", "please don't do that !" and also the words, "NO, NO, NO !". I was always told that, "you're getting on my nerves". Of course I didn't understand what nerves were so I didn't know what I was doing wrong.

STAGE 2

My teen years were great. I had no worries other than being dictated to by my parents and teachers as to the directions I should take in life. Life was fun. In those years I have many great memories of my many friends and the good ol' times.

STAGE 3

When I became a young adult I went to war. I was seventeen, almost at the end of my teen years. I enjoyed my U.S. Navy service in World War II even though the circumstances were not good.

True, our young adult years were completely different than today's young adult years, but that was then and this is now.

Scholastic training and the workplace took up my young adult years. It was a learning period for me with the wish I could achieve something though I didn't know what.

STAGE 4

By the time I reached middle age I knew where I was and felt in control of my future. I had a wife and child and my desires were settled as to my wants and desires. But then life took a turn and many things changed. Some of the changes were for the better and some for the worse but at no time was I not happy to enjoy the life I had been given.

I've always felt sorry for those people who can't laugh and enjoy each day no matter what bumps in the road they encounter.

Once middle age I wondered when I saw old people, how did they get that old. I never thought I'd reach that stage in life... but here I am OLD!

STAGE 5

I thought being old would be different from the earlier stages in life but there's no difference. Old age is just another stage in life and I'm enjoying every minute of it. The benefits are great.

You can tell people what you really think, do what you want, get your own way in so many different ways that makes your new stage 5 a pleasure to behold. You also find that people are courteous to you which makes you feel that you are one of the cherished few.

Most of all you can truly laugh at this new stage in life and make fun of yourself and the problems confronting you and the reactions of others towards you.

It's with these thoughts I had the idea of putting this book together.

In this book we've tried to give exaggerations and sometime truths of the many actions we older people sometimes think about, do and enjoy.

WHAT IT WAS LIKE IN MY EARLY DAYS

The father ruled the household.
Mothers stayed home and raised the family.
Children were to be seen and not heard.
Your hands, face and neck were checked for cleanliness at meals.
Dinner was announced with Mother stating, "Dinner's On"!
You had to sit straight at the dinner table and keep your elbows and hands off the table.
Cotton napkins and napkin rings were used at your place mat at meals and special linen napkins were only used for special occasions.
Young women were called "girls".
You never used bad language to express yourself.
When you were young you had to drink Ovaltine and take Cod Liver Oil regularly because "they are good for you".
Mothers had sewing kits and it was hard to wear something out since the minute there was a problem your Mother would repair the problem.
Children seldom went to restaurants with their parents.
You always addressed elders as; Miss, Mr. or Mrs.& never by their first name.
Boys can remember being photographed in a child's sailor suit.
When you lost a baby tooth the "Tooth Fairy" left a shiny penny under your pillow.
You used to bend down and pick up a penny 'cause it brought you good luck and it was also worth something.
Your home chores were taking in the milk from a metal box on the porch and helping to wash & dry the dishes after dinner.
The milkman delivered the milk in glass bottles and the milk was in the bottom part of the glass bottle while the cream was in the upper 'bubble' of the bottle which was sealed with a cardboard stopper. There was even a small metal spoon for removing the cream off the top of the bottle.
Orange juice was made by cutting an orange in half and pushing it on the grated upright in the middle of a flat green glass round unit.

You toasted bread on an electric toaster with two side panels that pulled away from the center unit with each side holding one piece of bread that you hoped would toast the bread the way you wanted it to.

Most homes had complete silver or silver plate serving sets for special occasions.

You went to your friends' apartments or houses to get together and there was never any parental worry.

One of your first paying jobs was having a newspaper route which was done by riding your bike with a front metal basket where you kept the rolled up newspapers that you'd throw on lawns or porches of those who'd subscribed to your paper.

Another job was selling magazines like Colliers, Ladies Home Journal, Saturday Evening Post, etc. for five cents from a cloth bag which held the magazines. You got paid for your work and in selling the magazines you collected "brownies" and "greenies" which you could trade in for prizes.

The work week was a full six days a week.

You thought FDR was going to be your President throughout your lifetime.

FDR's work programs including the NRA, WPA, TVA and others, plus his monetary regulatory programs which truly reversed the Depression and restored our country back to a normal economy.

Professional and laboring people had to serve apprenticeships before they became totally acceptable to practice and charge accordingly for their professional or trade expertise.

Girls joined the Brownies and The Girl Scouts Of America. Boys joined the Cub Scouts and The Boy Scouts Of America.

Doctors made house calls.

Quarantine signs had to be posted on apartment or house doors when an occupant got the measles, mumps or some other easily transmitted disease.

You could only have evening play time <u>after</u> finishing your homework and you had to be in bed at eight o'clock.

You looked forward to listening to your favorite nightly radio adventure series like the "Green Hornet" and "The Shadow"

before going to bed.
The family used to gather around the radio on Sunday nights to listen on the radio to the comedy shows by Fred Allen, Jack Benny, Joe Penner, Burns and Allen, Amos and Andy and others.
The radio was our only means of receiving any breaking news worldwide.

CLOTHES

Boys wore knickers to a certain early age and hated it.
Boys remembered how proud they were when they got their first pair of long trousers.
Men's pants were called "trousers".
Suspenders were called "braces".
Men wore three piece suits with vests in which they carried their gold pocket watches with gold watch fobs.
Women and girls always wore dresses or skirts with blouses but <u>never</u> wore trousers.
Women's and girls bathing suits covered a good part of their bodies.
Women wore girdles, corsets, garter belts and bloomers and women's nylon stockings came in two pieces.
Girls and women wore white gloves and patent shiny leather shoes with stockings on Sundays when going to church.
Men wore undershirts with shoulder straps.
Eye glasses were all metal framed.
Men had leather dress shoes for special occasions.
Boys had high-topped, leather-laced wintertime boots, which had a side pocket with a snap that held a folding pocket knife that came with the boots.
Boys had one pair of sneakers, then called "gym shoes" which were good for all sports but not for general use and they were mostly kept in lockers at whatever school you attended.
Jeans were called "dungarees" and they were all dark blue.

FOOD

Your mother used to buy her food at the local grocery store.
Grocery stores used to deliver food to your home without extra cost.
Fruits and vegetables didn't have preservatives and their shelf life was limited.
Food for the most part was regional.
Cracker Jack popcorn came in a big box with a good prize in the top of every box.
All medical, personal products, candies and gum were purchased from your local drugstore.
Drugstores also served ice cream sodas at their marble counters where there was a "Soda Jerk" who would make your favorite ice cream soda, banana split or sandwich.
There were round shaped different colored candies in a glass enclosed container that cost one penny. If you got a certain color candy it was worth a nickel or if really lucky you got a different color worth a dime.
Drive-in restaurants had waitresses in uniforms. They would take your food and soda orders and then return to your car and place the tray of food and drink on your turned down car door window. They got paid when serving you and got the tip when taking the tray for return.
Good Humor ice cream bars were purchased from their bell ringing trucks and if you got a 'lucky stick' it would state "FREE" on the wooden handle of your ice cream bar and you'd then get a free ice cream bar.
Flat packaged penny bubble gum included picture trading cards of Indians, Cowboys, Military Generals, Baseball Players and other notables with the pictured persons history on the back of each card.
Wrigley's chewing gum costs a penny.

APPLIANCES

Early on there was a change from the Ice Box in which you put large blocks of ice that were delivered to your home by the Iceman to the new Electric Refrigerators.

Ice Boxes didn't have freezing compartments nor did the newly introduced Refrigerators which replaced the Ice Box.

It took some time for people to call the new appliance by its rightful name.

The refrigerator was an odd looking unit and had a large circular ringed piping unit attached to the top of each machine.

There was always a glass jar filled with water in the refrigerator to cool water for drinking.

All home wiring was 110 volts and the wires were big and not color coordinated as they are today.

All homes were heated with iron radiators that had metal hoods (lids) that covered their tops.

Coal was first used to heat homes and you had to 'bank' the coals at night so the embers would stay lit 'til morning when you could then add more coal to get the fire to full blaze again.

Oscillating fans kept your family cool in the heat of summertime by fanning ice put in a shallow pan on the radiator hood while the family slept on the floor rug.

All houses and apartments had only one lock on their doors.

Washing clothes used to be done with a washing machine that had a wringer for getting as much of the water out of the clothes as possible. The women use to clean the clothes with a big bar of Borax soap which they used to scrub the clothes clean using a washboard.

All radios had to be plugged into a wall socket.

All cameras were either 120mm or 116mm and they only used black and white film.

You got a box camera as your first camera.

Phones were upright and black with rotary dials. They had hanging hearing units connected to a side holding arm for easy removal for listening to the person you were talking to and you talked into the circular mouthpiece in the front of the phone.

All phones were wire connected to a wall socket and they were all owned by the phone company.

All watches had jeweled interior works and kept time by winding their stems up daily.

Victrolas, as they were called, all had to be wound up and all records were 78rpm's.

SCHOOL

School teachers had dress codes; men wore suits and ties, women wore dresses.

You brought your lunch to school in a lunch box and always wanted to know what the dessert was.

You had your school desk where you put your books in the recessed area below the lid and each desk top had an ink well with an elongated recessed area where you kept your pens and pencils.

All school desks were made of a single construction combining wood with metal.

Your school pens had metal points called 'tibs' that had to be changed from time to time.

Wooden pencils were the writing instruments of choice.

All rulers were made of wood.

Schools had mimeograph gummy machines which wrote programs and exams printed on paper in light blue ink.

All typewriters were manual, heavy, black and had big keys.

Carbon paper was used in typewriters to make multiple copies and mistakes had to be erased with special ink erasers.

All school books were hardbound with black and white print.

Boys took 'Shop' and girls took 'Home Economics'.

SPORTS

Tennis racket frames were all made of wood.
Golf clubs shafts and heads were mostly made of wood.
Beginners ice skates had double runners that fit on shoes with a key.
Ice skates were high-topped shoes with ice skate blades attached to the bottom of the shoes.
Roller skates were all metal and you attached them to your shoes with a roller skate key.
Playing marbles was a big sport. Winning "aggies" or "bulleyes" were the best marbles you could win and the more marbles you won the more respected you were by your peers. This was a boy thing.
Girls played "hopscotch", "jump rope" and "jacks".
Boys and girls played, 1,2,3,4 Green Light...1,2,3,4 Red Light which was a form of hide and seek. "Green Light" meant you could <u>GO</u> and "Red Light" meant you had to <u>STOP</u> wherever you were.
Boys and girls also used to play, with closed fists, 1, 2, 3, 4, and then open their fists to either "rock", a "scissor", or a "paper". A paper won over a rock; a rock won over a scissor; a scissor won over a paper and so on.
Boys and girls used to play "knock-knock", "who's there?" like "Knock-knock". "Who's there?" "Boo". "Boo who?" "Sorry to hear you're sad!"
All bikes had only one speed, a wide flat seat, wide handlebars and you never owned a lock for your bike.
You went with your friends to any park to play marbles, hockey, baseball, football or whatever and always got a place to play.
Early boys and girls youth games were; musical chairs, spin the bottle, pin the tail on the donkey, checkers, pick-up sticks, horseshoes and scavenger hunts.
Decisions as what game to play sometimes was decided by going from person to person saying "eenie, meenie, minee, mo". The person whom "mo" wound up on then made the decision as to what game to play.

Making "cootie catchers" from one piece of paper and then telling someone they had "cooties" in their hair by showing them your "cootie catcher" used to be fun.
There were Duncan Yo-Yo contests and the winners were given a woolen sweater with a Duncan Yo-Yo Winner logo patch sewn on with the year of the win.
All boys had cap guns, yo-yo's, string wooden spinning tops, lead soldiers and comic books.
All girls had dolls, jump ropes, hopscotch chalk, jacks, and books.

TRANSPORTATION

All cars driven were made in the United States.
Cars were made of steel, had big front lights and a hood ornament with a water temperature gauge. Their interiors were adorned with linen material and curtains, had roll down windows with interior side lights, side flower holders, big front and back bumpers, large fenders and wide running boards with several round dials on their dashboards.
Early cars had to be "cranked-up" to start the motor.
Car horns always made an "ahooga" sound.
Coupes had "rumble" seats that could be closed or when opened they held two people.
Until 1932 all cars were straight 4 cylinder. They then changed to what we know as V8 cars. Today you can buy 4, 6, 8, 10 and more cylinder cars.
In the early days you could buy a new La Salle or Plymouth for $800 or a Packard for a slightly higher price.
Gas cost a nickel a gallon.
When you went into a gas station you could order 50 cents worth of gas and the attendant would wash your front and back windows, and check your oil.
Trolley cars with overhead wiring were in most towns and putting a shiny penny on the rails to "squish" them used to be fun.

Commercial planes were few.
Airports were only in a few metropolitan areas.
Only the rich and the daring flew anywhere.
There were no super highways.
Family vacations were mostly traveled by car or train.
Trains were all run by steam engines.
Going to Europe was only done by ship and only the wealthy could afford such trips.

ENTERTAINMENT

You went to the movies for a dime and saw the Pathe or Movietone News, a black & white "Betty Boop" cartoon followed by double feature movie with a continuing weekly adventure thriller movie which always left the hero hanging on a cliff or in some other precarious position. The thriller movie was always continued the following week. This was their way of having you come back to see how the hero would get out of his previous week's predicament.
All movies were black and white.
Spectacular movies had casts of thousands.
You went to drive-in-movies where you parked your car on a slant next to speaker hung on an upright which you placed on your turned down car window sill so you and your occupants could hear the movie.
All dance bands had twelve or more members. It was the era of the big bands.
There were small square thick adventure books series about the Hardy Boys and even Dick Tracy. They had black and white text with black and white line drawings. Circa 1930's.
There were "Nancy Drew" mystery series books for girls.
All Sunday newspapers had a comic section that first went to the parents and then were passed to the children.
Some comic strips forecast the future like the Dick Tracy cartoon with his two way radio watch and Flash Gordon and Buck Rogers with their space ships to the moon and beyond.

In New York City Mayor LaGuardia became well known for reading the Sunday comics on the radio every week to the children of New York City. He was also one of the most loved Mayors of his day.

CHANGES IN TODAY'S WORLD THAT ARE TAKEN FOR GRANTED

MODERN TRANSPORTATION

Today's cars have changed in almost every way.
Yesterday's cars had the fundamental ability of going forward and backward and were made of steel. When the manufacturers changed to making cars of lighter metals many jokes were made about the new unsafe lighter cars.
Nevertheless, today's cars made of even lighter materials have: safety seat belt constraints, front seat and steering wheel adjustment controls, air conditioning, two zone temperature controls, radio button controls in the front and back seat areas, back seat area TV units, outside temperature and directional viewing units, air safety bags in the front seat area and the door sides, open roof controls, automatic trunk opener, outside numbered control panel for opening or locking your doors, stereo controls for CD's and tapes and many other appointments that were not even thought of in the early days.
Today's cars' components are chip driven and come in a selection of 4, 6, 8, 10 and even more cylinders.
My expertise in this area of evaluation is nil other than driving a car and hoping I don't meet someone on the road who has "Road Rage" which is today's title for the mentally unhinged behind the wheel of a car.

TRAINS

Riding trains in yesterday's world was fun.
Today's trains are run by diesel and electric engines while the earlier trains were run by steam engines.

In the old days you could hear the clickity-clack of the rails when traveling.
Going first class you either had an upper or lower berth that was sheltered by a green hanging curtain with a number on it. If you wanted your shoes shined you left them in the aisle when you went to bed and the Porter shined your shoes at night and left them in the aisle in front of your berth in the morning.
Today's trains have separate compartments shielded with locking doors and home-like appointments which gives the occupants total privacy and comfort.
The only negative riding by train today is not hearing the clickity-clack of the rails.

FLYING

Flying used to be for the wealthy and daring.
Planes were all prop controlled and didn't hold the number of passengers that today's planes hold.
Airports were fewer which limited the areas you could fly to and from.
Major cities was where the main airport hubs existed. Now you can fly to many airports in every state and fly to almost every country in the world.
Flying is now routine for anyone who wishes to expedite their traveling from point A to point B.
The relative safety and comfort zone in flying has changed and is no longer for the daring and wealthy alone. In fact so many people are now flying that today's airplane industry is having trouble booking all their flights and are asking the government to let them install additional runways to help them keep pace with their growing demand.

CLOTHING

In the old days when you went out to dinner or any social event with friends you always dressed up. This was especially true when traveling on vacation.

In today's world most travelers on vacation dress down for comfort.

Missing from today's men's attire are summertime straw hats, wintertime regular brimmed hats, vests, pocket watches, collar clips, tie clips, cuff links, argyle socks and penny loafers with real shining pennies which you placed in the center of each shoe.

Watches as we knew them have also changed. When you look at your watch today you can do all types of math, get the weather, talk to friends while also get the time, day and date. There's even talk about going on the Web with your watch. Today's watches have changed completely and are mostly run by Quartz movements.

Women's clothing I don't think has changed that much other than the type of fabrics used. The garment industry makes yearly changes in fashion to keep the women buying the new designs in order to keep their industry flourishing.

I find it amusing to see women's dress designs which are the return of yesterday's fashion statements which their industry keeps reinventing.

The funniest fashion statements of today's world are made by the youth. How anybody can walk in the jeans that some of the youth wear is something I can't figure out. The youth wear jeans with the crotch down to their knees and their backside underwear showing while the bottom of their jeans slop on the ground. Walking in those jeans must pose a challenge in many ways but I guess that's the fun of wearing them the way they do.

When we were young we wore what our parents told us to wear.

SHOES

This is a fun area. I say this because when I was young we had one pair of "sneakers", then called "gym shoes" that were good for every sport and activity. They were made by Keds and were either flat or of high-topped design.

Today they make sneakers for all sorts of weather conditions and all types of sports. They have sneakers that light-up when you walk and they just came out with sneakers that make a "boink" noise when you walk or run.

I pity the poor child whose parents can't afford a one hundred dollar plus pair of sport sneakers for their children or for the new styles of just invented sneaker the manufacturers keep inventing. They even have special sneakers made just for walking down the street with friends.

There are so many type of sneakers made today that a parent could easily spend a fortune for their children's sneakers alone.

Dress shoes for men in leather are pretty much the same although I now see different type of leisure shoes that are being worn and accepted as dress shoes.

Women's shoe industry has changed. They have different materials and styles that I for one don't truly understand. Some of today's styles make a women taller by having klutzy soles manufactured on the bottom of the shoes. They also have some styles you can actually 'hear'.

When walking down a street one day I heard this loud rhythmic clicking sound only to look back and see this women with elevated shoes with some type of very hard heel tips that banged with each step the women took. Don't know if it was a protective measure on her part or a fashion statement she wanted everyone to see and hear.

TOILETRIES

In terms of men's toiletries, men's straight razors, their sharpening blade straps, wooden lather containers and lather brushes are no longer in use except at some barber shops. The new triple bladed edged Gillette razors are in. There are also disposable razors for those in need. Shaving cream has now been put in a can for easy dispensing.

Deodorants have also changed. We didn't have roll-ons, pads and seven day deodorants. I also think this is good since more men and women are now knowledgeable about the use of deodorants for which I am thankful.

OFFICE MACHINES

This is an area where everything has changed. Everyone has computers 'cept delivery boys who have Pagers. The electric typewriter is almost a dead entity, though I do have a fifty year old Hermes manual typewriter which I used when I started a business some years back. Admittedly if I had to use that same typewriter today I couldn't since my fingers have been spoiled through the use of computers.

Fax machines are new..Computers are new..Color Printers are new..Scanners are new..Speakers with Computers are new.. the Web is new..all sorts of software are new..hand held Palm units are new..Cell phones are new..portable telephones are new..Pagers are new..in fact almost everything used in offices and businesses are new except for the people working with them.

Today's phones have; touch tone, hold, call waiting, volume control, speaker phone ability, redial, locator/intercom, change of channels options, plus portability and multiple styling. You can also own your own phone. They also come in an unbelievable assortment of styles.

Today's office is one area that is almost impossible to keep pace with. It's truly a whole new technology era and area.

MEDICAL

I'll not even attempt to delve into this area other than to say that if a person needs a new hip, heart, liver, lung, knee, kidney, pancreas or some other body part there is a chance they might be able to get the replacement part wanted.

There have been so many advancements in the medical profession that it is my belief this area alone is most beneficial for mankind in this new technological era of ours for doctors, patients and society as a whole.

HOUSEHOLD

Today's children seem to dictate policy to their elders. They tell them what they want and when they want it. This starts with the meals and ends with the clothing.
In the old days the parents dictated how they wanted their children to dress, behave, get good grades and only upon following the dictates of their parents were the children given an allowance _if_ money was available. A big allowance was a quarter.
Yes, time have changed in many ways and though people are physically the same their attitudes and focus seems to be different.

Most changes have been for the better so is it a good time to be alive, you bet it is and always will be.

Things are different to our older generation but there will always be differences with every new generation.
Just think of the many changes the next generation will be able to look back on.

What we've tried to do with the cartoons that follow is to give an exaggeration and sometimes truths of the many actions we older people sometime think about, do and enjoy with laughter.
It is our hope that our following cartoons opens a door for you regarding the enjoyment we older people have, sometimes laughing at ourselves and at other times laughing at others who laugh at us. With luck you too will be able to enjoy your later years in life. Remember, it's just another stage in life and it's fun.

CARTOON TIME...

YOU CAN ALWAYS WORK AS A NIGHT WATCHMAN!

DO YOU THINK WORKING HERE WOULD MAKE YOU FEEL YOUNGER?

I CAME UP THE HARD WAY FOR VERY LITTLE MONEY.
NOW PLEASE REPEAT YOUR DESIRES.

YOUR THIRTY YEARS RESUME IS GREAT - BUT WE'LL HAVE TO START YOU IN OUR RETAIL SALES DEPARTMENT

NOW I'M CONVINCED I SHOULD HAVE RETIRED!

YOUR GENERATION HAD IT EASY!

IT'S HARD TO BELIEVE THEY'RE PART OF OUR GENERATION!

YOU'RE 70?!

YOU USED TO BE A LOVER, NOW YOU'RE A LETCH!

WILL YOU EVER STOP COMPLAINING ABOUT MY EATING HABITS.

'DON'T WORRY, HE CAN'T TELL YOU NEED A HEARING AID.

HONEY, NOW CAN YOU HEAR ME?

YOU'VE NEVER SEEN GRANDCHILDREN MORE BEAUTIFUL THAN MINE!

GIRLS, LET'S SHARE THE COST OF THE MEALS ON THIS TRIP.

NOW THAT I CAN AFFORD TO EAT ANYTHING I WANT... I CAN'T!

REMEMBER, WE'RE YOUR ONLY LIVING RELATIVES!

YOU BOTH LOOK GREAT!
WE'LL KEEP IN TOUCH -
NEED ANY HELP JUST GIVE US A RING...

POPS, ARE WE ALL IN YOUR WILL?

LIVING IN RETIREMENT MUST BE FUN?

YOU GUYS DON'T MIND BABYSITTING YOUR GRANDCHILDREN FOR A FEW WEEKS, DO YOU?

COULD YOU GROCERY SHOP FOR ME TO HELP FILL YOUR DAY?

CAN YOU TAKE CARE OF MY CATS WHILE I'M ON VACATION?

DON'T YOU THINK THAT'S A BIT RACY FOR YOU?

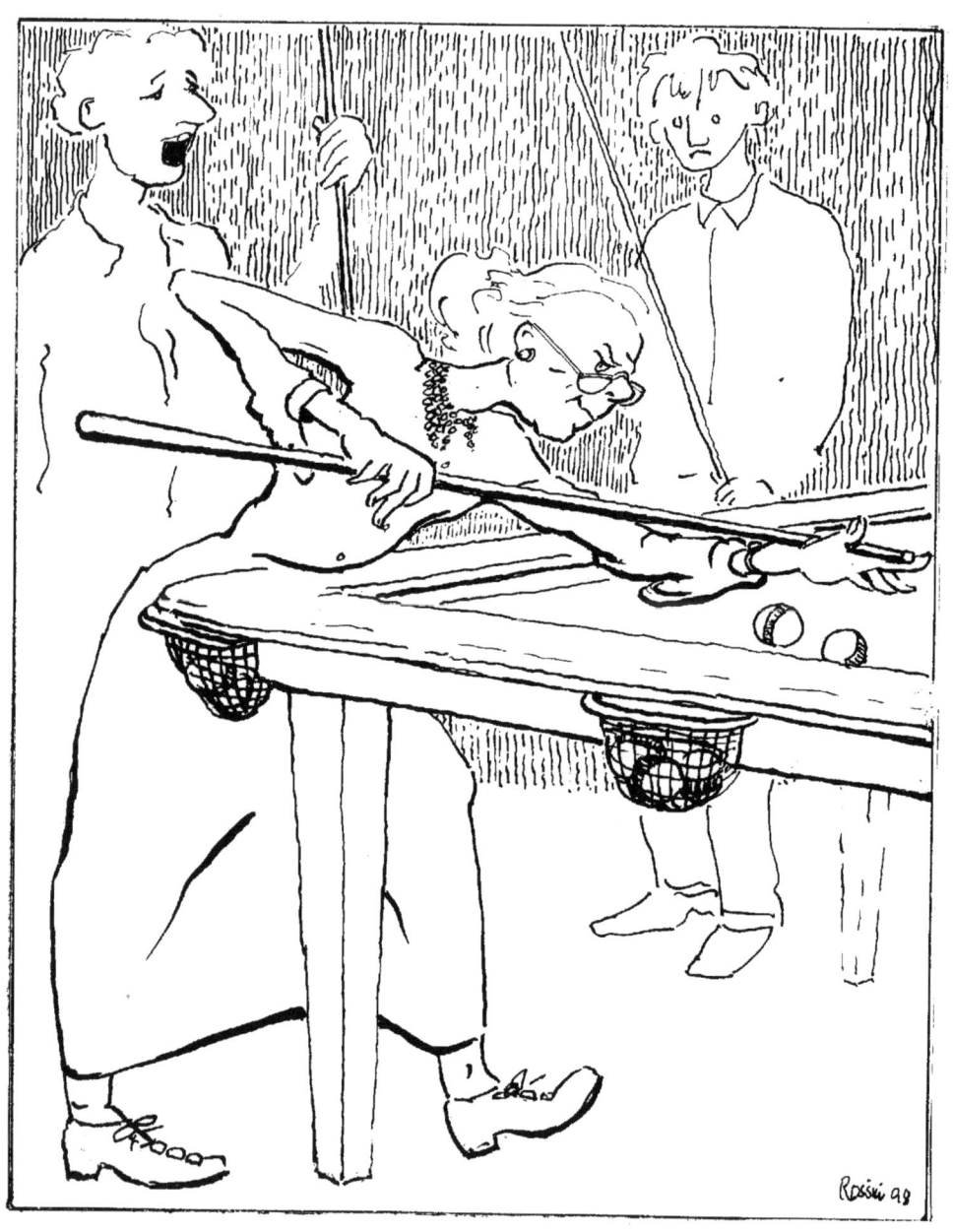

I THOUGHT YOUR GRANDMOTHER NEVER PLAYED THIS GAME?

DON'T WORRY ABOUT SPORTS, YOU CAN ALWAYS PLAY GOLF.

HOW MUCH FURTHER, CAN'T WE STOP FOR ICE CREAM?

WOW. YOU PROMISED TO TAKE IT EASY, GRAMPS!

**GRAMPS YOU PROMISED TO TEACH US -
NOT SHOW OFF!**

WATCH OUT FOR HARRY. HE HAS A HABIT OF FALLING ASLEEP AT THE WHEEL.

WILL WE LOOK LIKE THAT SOME DAY?

POPS, EVER GET THE FEELING YOUR LIFE'S BEHIND YOU?

DAD FOR HEAVEN'S SAKE, ACT YOUR AGE!

DID YOU REALLY HAVE A LOT OF HAIR?

NEED ANY HELP DAD?

AND WE THOUGHT YOU'D NEVER MAKE IT!

DID YOU EVER THINK IT WOULD COME TO THIS?

BERTHA, WELCOME ABOARD AGAIN. OF COURSE I REMEMBER YOU, HOW COULD I FORGET YOU?

DO YOU THINK HE HAS ULTERIOR MOTIVES?

HIS NEW MARRIAGES ALWAYS SEEM TO PEP HIM UP.

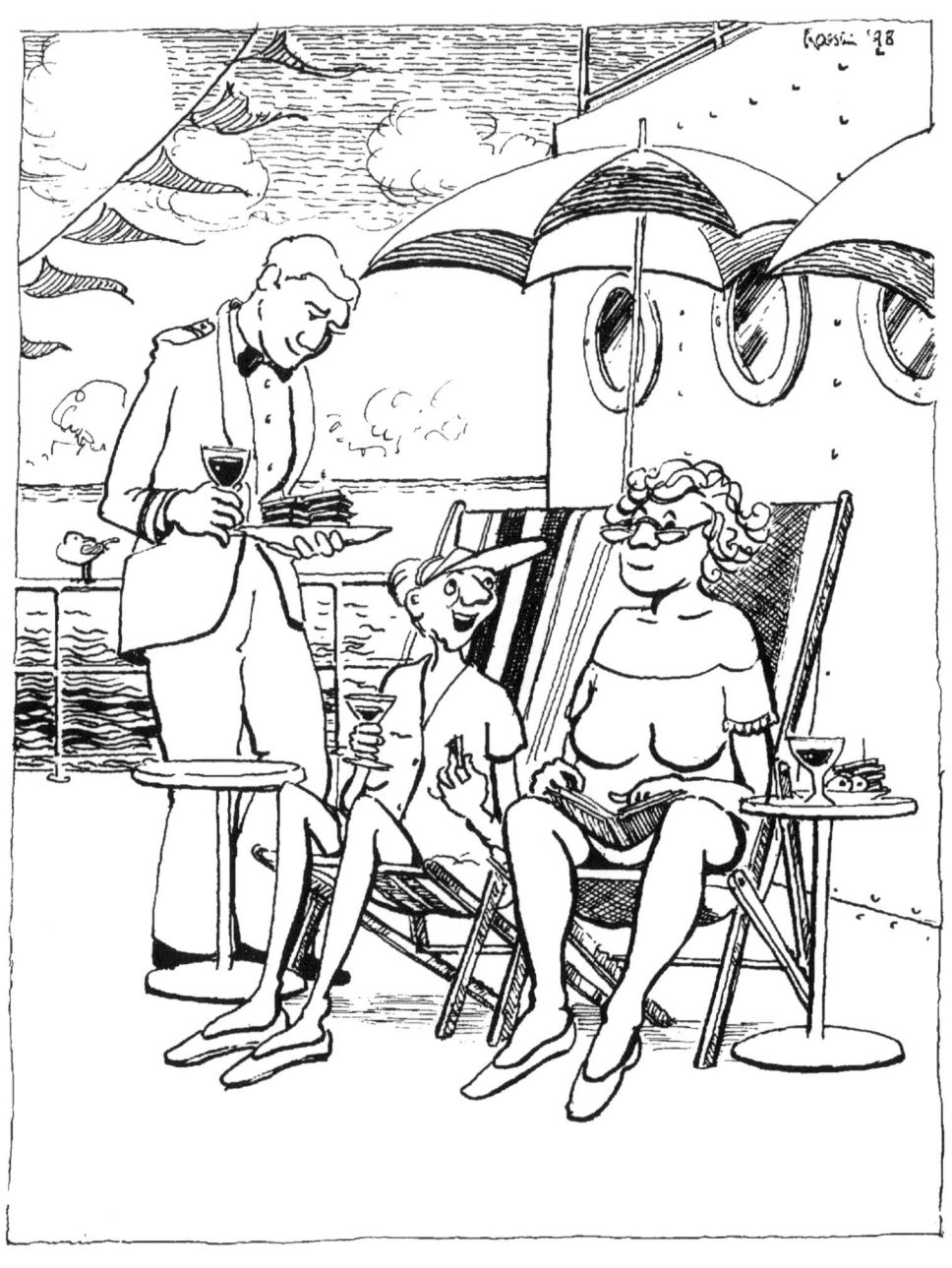

AND WHEN DID YOUR HUSBAND DIE?

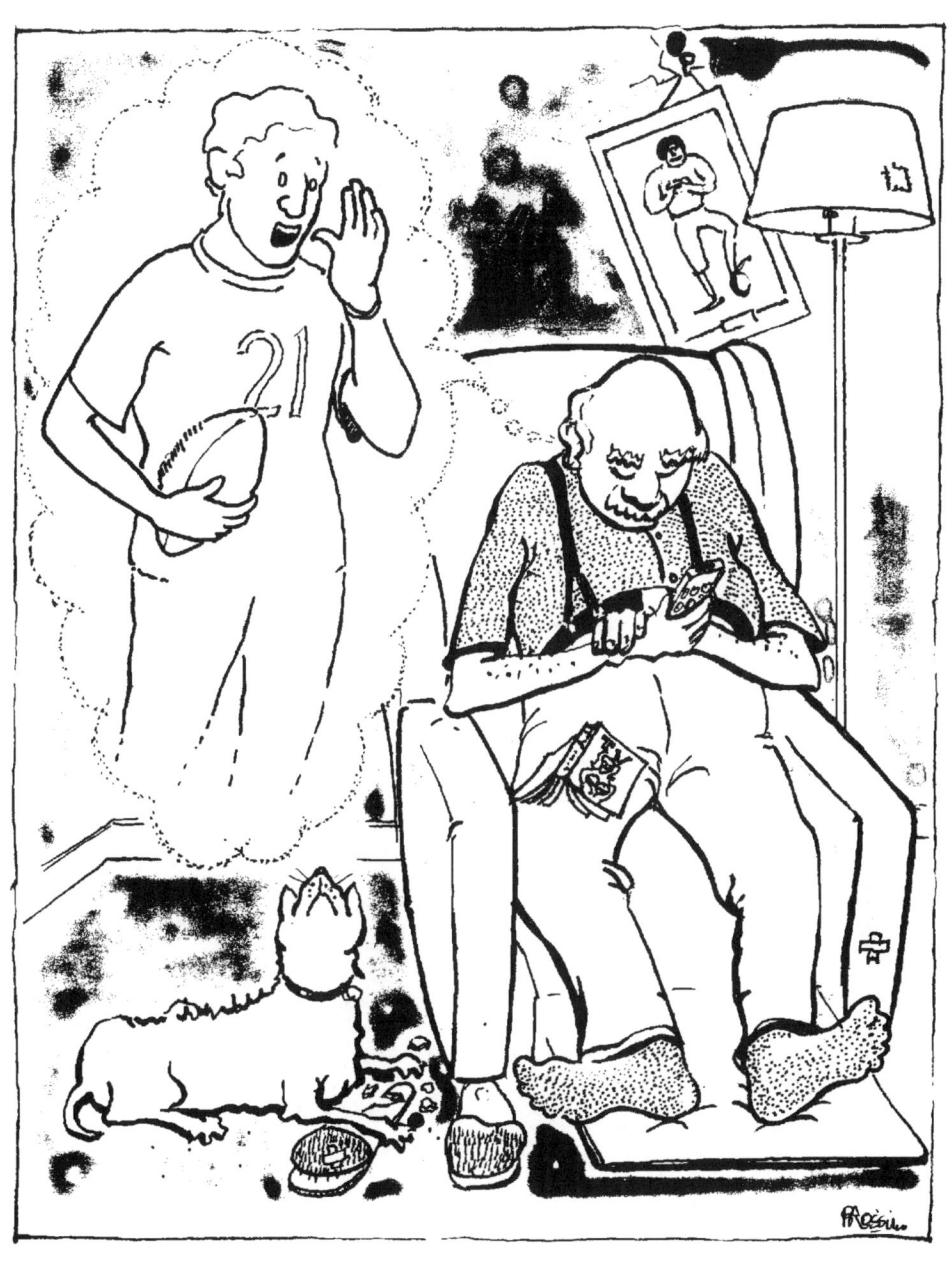

FOR EVERY OLD PERSON THERE'S A YOUNG PERSON WANTING TO RETURN.

LOOKING IN THE MIRROR AND SEEING A STRANGER.

YOU REALLY ARE IN GOOD SHAPE FOR A PERSON OF YOUR AGE.

I THOUGHT OF YOU YESTERDAY BUT I DIDN'T KNOW IF YOU WERE STILL WITH US.

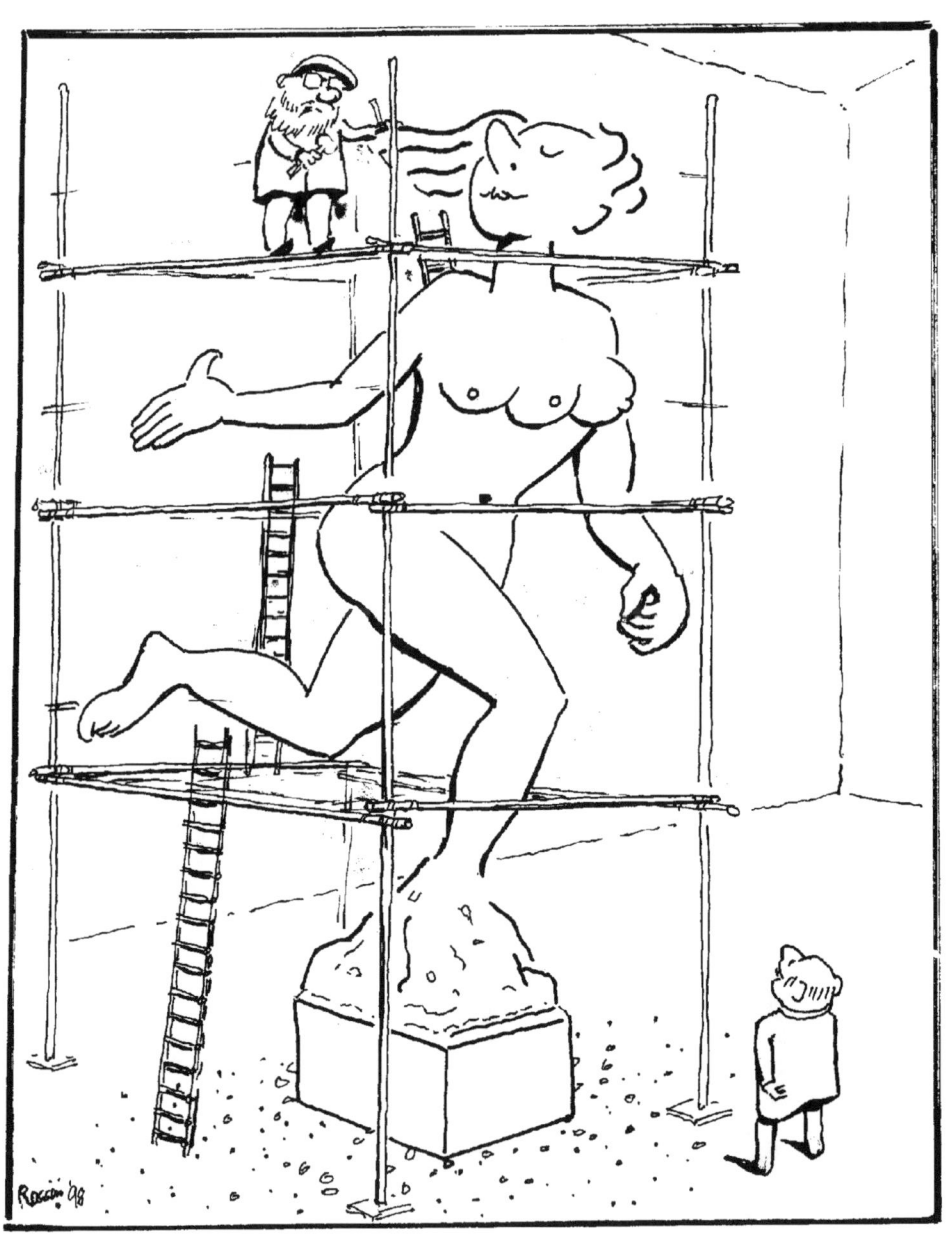

FRED, YOU'RE BECOMING FORGETFUL!

AT WHAT AGE DID YOU START BECOMING FORGETFUL?

IT'S THE THIRD TIME THIS WEEK YOU'VE TRIED TO SHORT CHANGE ME.

HARRY, I TOLD YOU TO HAVE THAT OPERATION!

IF YOU HAVE A TOUCH-TONE PHONE PLEASE PRESS #1.
IF YOU NEED ACCOUNTS PAYABLE PLEASE PRESS #2,
IF YOU NEED A PRIMARY PHYSICIAN PLEASE PRESS ....

YOUR LUCKY THEY'VE GOT SO MANY SPARE PARTS IN TODAY'S WORLD.

REPLACE WHAT? DOCTOR, I FEEL LIKE AN OL' USED CAR.

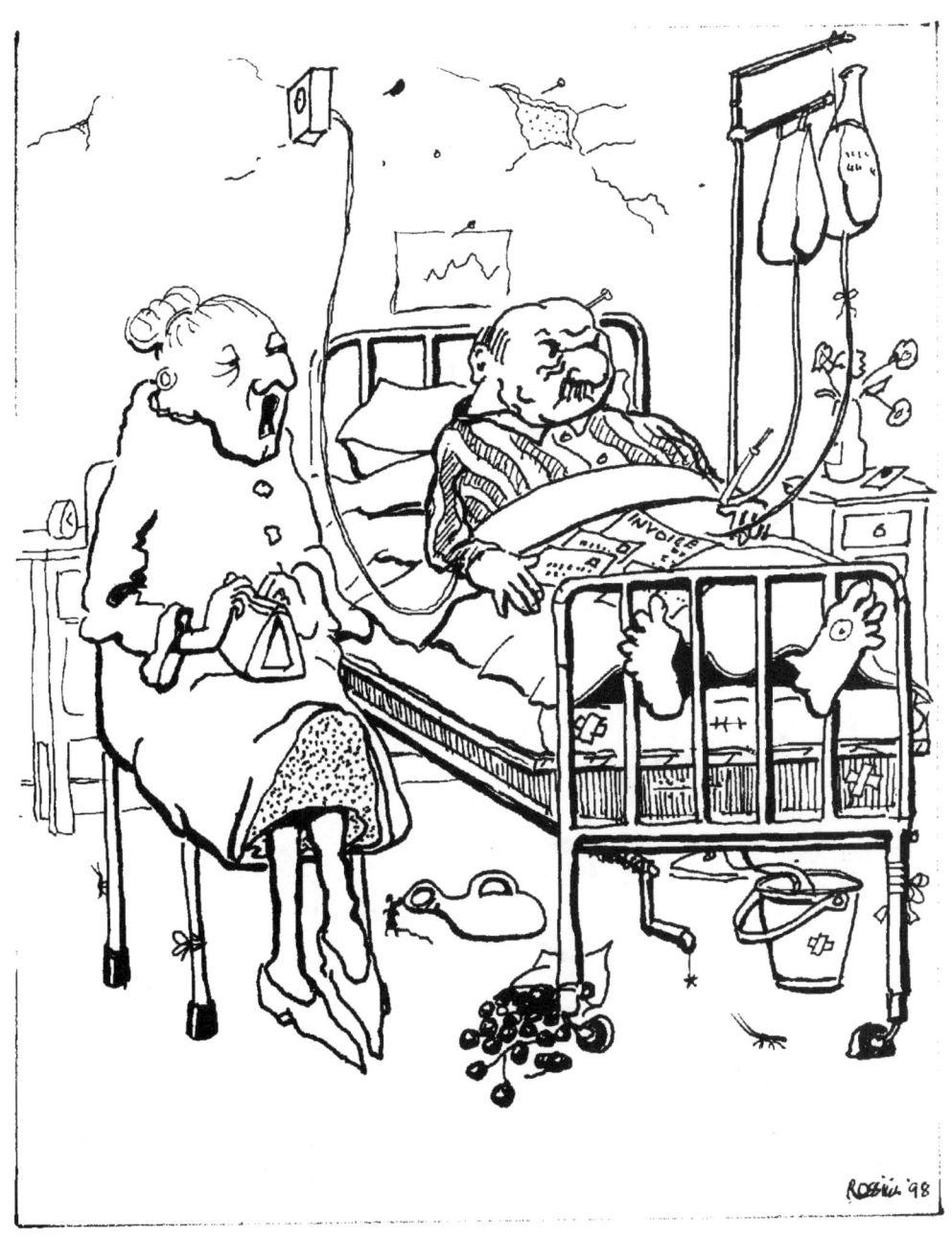

I KNOW YOU FEEL BADLY BUT IT'S BETTER THAN THE ALTERNATIVE.

HAVE YOU ALWAYS BEEN FRIGHTENED OF DENTISTS?

YOU'RE EXPECTED TO PUT ON WEIGHT AT YOUR AGE.

READY FOR PHYSICAL THERAPY?

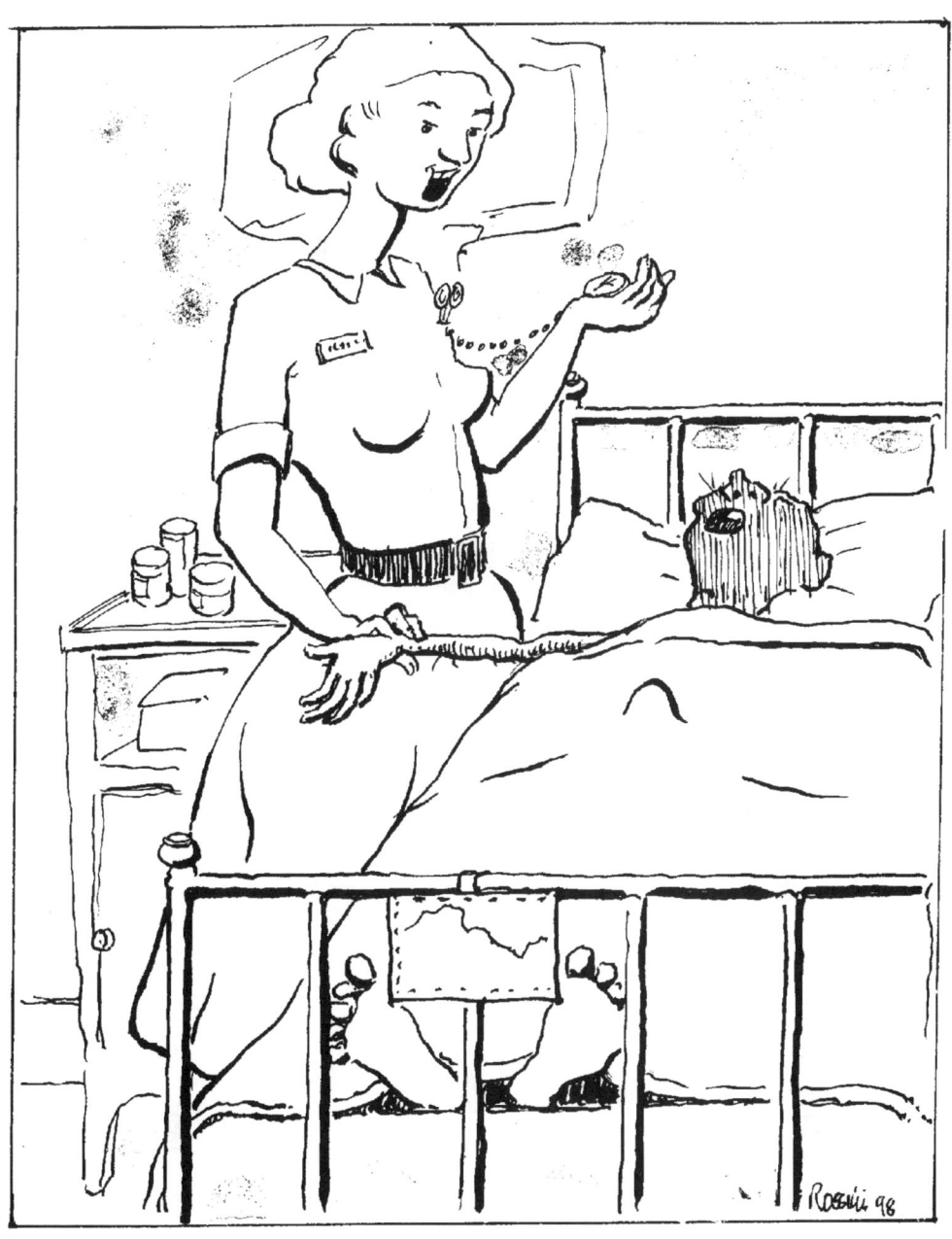

YOU'LL BE HAPPY TO KNOW YOUR VITAL SIGNS ARE FINE.

I THINK IT'S TIME NOW WE LOOKED IN ON MR. JONES.

DON'T YOU THINK IT'D BE WISE TO FINALLY GET A HEARING AID?

POOR OLD DEVIL. HIS SENSE OF SMELL LEFT HIM
LATER IN LIFE.

GOOD LOOKING AS HE IS, ARE ALL HIS PARTS IN WORKING ORDER?

DON'T YOU THINK A LIGHTER SHADE OF BLUE WOULD HAVE BEEN MORE FLATTERING?

TOUPEES ARE FLATTERING, YOU KNOW.

HE TAKES EVERY OPPORTUNITY TO SHOW OFF HIS NEW TEETH!

YOUR NEW DENTAL WORK IS REALLY BLINDING.

WHEN DID YOU LAST SEE YOUR TEETH?

DID YOU AND GRAM ENTERTAIN LIKE THIS ONCE?

FRED'S ALWAYS THE FIRST TO LEAVE OUR LITTLE GATHERINGS.

FEELING INVISIBLE AT FAMILY GATHERINGS.

I TOLD YOU WE SHOULD'VE STARTED THE SENIOR PARTY EARLIER.

YOU REALLY WERE PRETTY BACK THEN!

YOU LOOK BETTER NOW THAN WHEN YOU WERE YOUNGER.

WE LIKE YOUR PRESERVES BUT WE'RE USED TO THE STORE BOUGHT KIND.

SORRY DAD, BUT I'VE BEEN TOO BUSY TO CALL YOU.

WERE YOU REALLY AS YOUNG AS ME ONCE?

POPS, DO YOU STILL HAVE A SEX LIFE?

HEY POPS, NOW'S THE TIME YOU SHOULD BE ENJOYING LIFE.

DAD, AREN'T YOU TOO OLD TO BE DOING THAT?

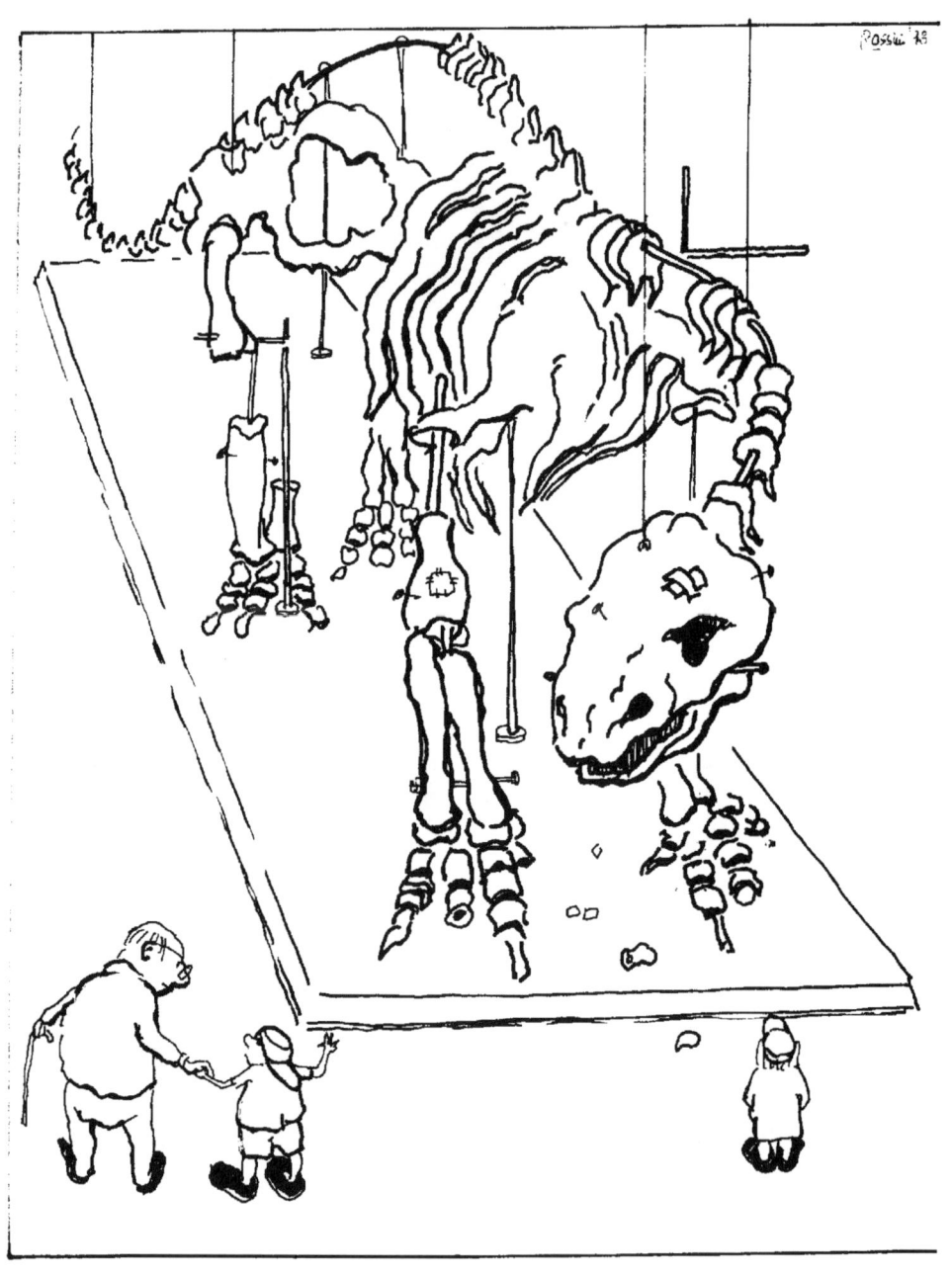

GRANDPA, WERE THEY REALLY THAT BIG?

HOW FAR BACK CAN YOU REMEMBER?

THANKS FOR THE CALL, BUT I REALLY CAN'T USE A DIAPER SERVICE.

THANKS, BUT I REALLY DON'T WANT MAGAZINE SUBSCRIPTIONS.

HAVE YOU THOUGHT OUT A DIVISION OF YOUR PROPERTY YET?

BEING OLD REALLY HAS ITS REWARDS.

I KEEP TELLING HIM TO CUT THE GRASS BEFORE HIS LUNCHTIME DRINK.

I'M GLAD YOU'VE FINALLY FOUND SOMETHING TO TINKER WITH.

SINCE RETIREMENT THIS PROJECT OF HIS
HAS OCCUPIED A LOT OF HIS TIME.

DO YOU MISS THE GOOD OL' DAYS?

WILLARD THINKS HE'S HOT STUFF!

I JUST WISH ONCE, THEY'D ASK ME MY AGE AGAIN.

POOR HENRY HAS GOTTEN SO OLD!

WOULD YOU LIKE TO TAKE MY SEAT, SIR?

CAN'T YOU EVER REMEMBER WHERE YOU LEFT THE CAR KEYS?

I USED TO BE A LOT TALLER!

I'M JUST A SHADOW OF MY FORMER SELF.

RECEIVING AVALANCHES OF MAIL THAT WOULD MAKE ANYONE FEEL OLD.

I WISH THEY'D MAKE THE OBITS PRINTING LARGER.

DON'T ANSWER THAT, IT'S DEATH-KNELL HARRY WITH THE LATEST OBIT.

CAN YOU MAKE IT TO THE STORE TODAY?

THEY SAY AFTERNOON NAPS ARE GOOD FOR YOU.

YOU'D SLEEP BETTER IF YOU TOOK LESS NAPS- AND SO WOULD I !

DO COME IN FOR TEA, THEY JUST LOOK MEAN.

DON'T YOU FEEL THE WORLD IS PASSING US BY?

DO YOU THINK YOU SHOULD REALLY WEAR THAT AT YOUR AGE?

I BET YOU'VE ALWAYS BEEN A FASHION LEADER.

I'M NOT SO LONELY I CAN'T GIVE YOU AWAY.

AREN'T WE SUPPOSED TO BE TAKING IT EASY AT OUR AGE?

UNTIL YOU'RE RETIRED, YOU DON'T REALIZE THE STRESS.

DID YOU CONFUSE OUR FLIGHTS AGAIN?

NOW THAT HURRICANE ADOLPH IS OVER, LET'S RETIRE BACK TO NEW ENGLAND.

IT'S NOT YOUR HEARING OR YOUR AGE, IT'S YOUR ATTITUDE.

I GET A BETTER GREETING FROM THEM THAN I GET FROM MY RELATIVES.

THESE HEADSTONES CARRY A LIFETIME GUARANTEE.

I'M GOING TO BE CREAMATED. DO YOU HAVE ANYTHING IN CARDBOARD?

AND THEY SAY YOU CAN'T TAKE IT WITH YOU.

GRANDDAD, WHAT'S AN OL' FOLKS HOME?

EVERYBODY LOVES OUR GOURMET FOOD.

WE HAVE WHEELCHAIR RACES IN THE SUMMERTIME.

DAD, YOU'LL MEET MANY NEW FRINDS HERE.

WE'LL VISIT YOU EVERY DAY!

WELL PAUL, IT LOOKS AS THOUGH WE'VE FINALLY FINISHED OUR LITTLE BOOK. HOPE IT BRINGS A SMILE OR TWO TO ITS READERS.